The Bible Speaks to Me
About My Beliefs

The Bible Speaks to Me About My Beliefs

by
W. E. McCumber

Beacon Hill Press of Kansas City
Kansas City, Missouri

ISBN: 083-411-285X

Printed in the
United States of America

Cover: Royce Ratcliff

10   9   8   7   6   5   4   3   2   1

Contents

Preface

To attempt a poor man's biblical theology within the compass of these pages is a mission impossible. I can only hope to whet the reader's appetite for further study in larger and better volumes on the subject.

The severe limitations of space became frustrating. Too much material clamored for inclusion, and shutting the door against it was difficult. I began to feel like the man who grabbed a lion and begged for someone to help him turn it loose.

I am indebted to many teachers, none of whom may wish to have their names associated with my efforts to articulate the message of the Bible in some of its more salient doctrines. I am equally indebted to many students and congregations with whom I have shared much of this material in various forms. From them I learned more than I taught.

A lifelong engagement with the Bible has been a labor of love. My hope and prayer is that all who read this little book will find their interest in, and appreciation for, the Bible strengthened and enlarged.

William Lyon Phelps has been quoted as saying, "You can learn more about human nature by reading the Bible than by living in New York." And you can learn more about God by reading the Bible than by living anywhere except heaven. I hope, therefore, that this book about the Bible will incite more reading of the Bible itself. No other book conveys God's saving truth to a world desperately in need of salvation.

1

The Speaking Book

The Bible speaks to us about our beliefs.

That one sentence is this whole book in a nutshell. Everything you will read in these pages is based squarely upon the premise contained in the eight simple words that form this proposition: *The Bible speaks to us about our beliefs.*

Let us begin by giving our attention to the Bible as a speaking book. Before we examine *what* it says, let us concentrate on the fact *that* it says. As the Word of God, the Bible is unique among all the literature of earth.

The Bible, the entire Bible, and nothing but the Bible is finally authoritative for the faith and life of Christians. To believe what the Bible affirms and to practice what the Bible commands is the first and foremost responsibility of every follower of Jesus Christ.

The reason for this is simple and clear: The Bible tells us what we need to know about God, about ourselves, and about what God has done to save us from sin and to unite us with himself forever. The oft-quoted words of John Wesley deserve repeating here:

> I am a spirit come from God, and returning to God: just hovering over the great gulf, till, a few moments hence, I am no more seen; I drop into an unchangeable eternity! I want to know one thing—the way to heaven; how to land safe on that happy shore.

God himself has condescended to teach the way; for this very end He came from heaven. He hath written it down in a book. O give me that book! At any price, give me the book of God! I have it: here is knowledge enough for me. Let me be *homo unius libri* [a man of one book].

I. THE BIBLE SPEAKS . . .

A. *More precisely put, God speaks through the Bible. The Bible is God's Word.*

When we read the Bible we are not aware of being addressed from the past by its human authors. We are conscious, rather, of being addressed in the present by its divine Author. We do not hear Moses, Isaiah, John, or Paul issuing commands and making promises. What we are acutely aware of is God himself speaking—calling us, claiming us, commanding us, comforting us. The Bible is *God's* Word.

To say this is not to deny the human writers, known and unknown, or to obscure their differences in personality, outlook, and style. The Bible is the Word of God *in the words of men.* The men differed from one another in many ways, but they all had this in common—that God chose them, equipped them, and inspired them to write. As Simon Peter expressed it, referring specifically to prophetic portions of Scripture: "No prophecy ever came by the impulse of man, but men moved by the Holy Spirit spoke from God" (2 Pet. 1:21).

When quoting Old Testament passages, the apostles sometimes named their human writers. Preaching at Pentecost, for example, Peter began a quotation with the words, "This is what was spoken by the prophet Joel" (Acts 2:16). He began another quotation, "For David says" (2:25). However, another

10

New Testament preacher begins a quotation from Psalm 95 with the phrase "as the Holy Spirit says" (Heb. 3:7).

The apostles did not regard these different ways of prefacing quotations as contradictory. Behind the different human writers was the one divine Author who inspired their writings. Therefore, the Bible was not regarded as the opinions and speculations of men, however wise and good those men were. The Bible was—and is—the Word of God.

This is so true that sometimes neither the human writers nor the divine Author are mentioned. Instead, for example, John quotes an Old Testament prophet but introduces the quotation with the phrase "scripture says" (John 19:37). And Paul writes, "Scripture says to Pharaoh" (Rom. 9:17). He refers to a message that had reached Pharaoh, not as a written word (scripture) but as a *spoken* word from Moses. This message was recorded later, after the death of Pharaoh. Evidently, the apostles regarded the phrases "God says" and "the Bible says" as synonymous. They believed that God speaks through the Bible.

B. *This does not mean that bits of Scripture snatched out of context are God's Word to us.*

When tempting Christ, the devil misused Scripture in this way. Along he came, the arrogant rascal, with a Bible in his hand and sounding like a preacher. Jesus had just parried one temptation by quoting Scripture: "It is written . . ." Now Satan tried to buttress a second temptation with a passage from Psalms, but he yanked it out of context and gave it a false application. It was not, *as he used it,* God's word to Jesus. The Lord brushed it aside, therefore, and quoted another passage, rightly applied, to defeat the devil.

We need to say, then, that the Bible, *when accurately quoted*

11

and honestly applied, is God's Word to us. What is written in one part of Scripture must be interpreted in the light of all that Scripture says on that particular subject. The Bible is truth revealed, but it is not to be treated like a magic charm.

II. THE BIBLE SPEAKS TO US . . .

A. *The Bible as God's Word means the Bible as personal address.*

This is how we must hear the Bible's message if we are to benefit from its purpose.

Some schools offer courses in "The Bible as Literature," and such courses are not without value. But the Bible viewed merely as a body of ancient literature has no redeeming power. The Bible as an object at our disposal, to be analyzed in a cool, clinical manner, will no more save us from sin and unite us to God than will a reading of *Robinson Crusoe, Great Southern Cooking,* or the Chicago telephone directory. The Bible as literature may interest, but it does not save.

In the same way, to read the Bible as history only, or as sociology only, in order to study its influence upon other times and places and people, frustrates its real intent. Whatever effect the Bible had upon our great-great-great-grandfathers, it can only exert a saving impact upon us when we listen to its message as God's Word to us—directly, powerfully, and inescapably to us.

Jesus once said to certain first-century listeners, "Unless you repent you will all likewise perish" (Luke 13:3). That means nothing until we hear it as a summons to us, a warning that we must repent or we will perish.

Jesus said to Nicodemus, "You must be born anew" (John 3:7). That means nothing to us if we merely overhear it as a snatch of conversation between a first-century itinerant rabbi and a puzzled member of the Jewish Sanhedrin. Only as it comes to us as the Lord's word, comes to us as command and promise, will it open the gates of the kingdom of God.

John wrote to a congregation under his apostolic supervision, "The blood of Jesus his Son cleanses us from all sin" (1 John 1:7). That has no meaning for us until we hear it as the promise of our redemption and our holiness.

The Bible is more than history, poetry, law, biography, philosophy, and sociology. The Bible is *God's Word*, contemporary with us, coming to us, making its disclosure to us, imposing its demands on us, offering us salvation, and promising us forgiveness, cleansing, renewal, and peace. Unless we hear it in this way we have not really heard it at all.

For this reason, a person may know a lot about the Bible without deriving benefit from the Bible. In a Tennessee town years ago, I met a carpenter who knew a lot about the Bible, and he was eager to display that knowledge. He knew how many books, chapters, verses, and words the Bible contains. He knew the longest verse, the shortest verse, the middle verse. He knew the longest chapter, the shortest chapter, the longest book, the shortest book. He knew how many times the word *God* appeared in the Bible. He could name in order the books of the Old Testament and the New Testament. He could name many of the Bible characters and recite stories about them. When it came to mechanical information he was a walking Bible encyclopedia—a strutting one actually.

When I questioned him about his personal relationship to Jesus Christ, however, he admitted that he was not a Christian. He was a slave to his sins, and the whole purpose of God in giving us the Bible had thus far eluded him. To him the Bible was an object of intellectual curiosity; he did not hear it as God's personal address to him.

This does not mean that God was not speaking to him through the Bible. It only means that he was not listening. We cannot determine the nature and contents of the Bible; those are *given*. The Bible is what it claims to be—the Word of God—whether we hear it or not, whether we believe it or not. But we do determine what the Bible is *to us*. The Bible only becomes the Word of God that saves us when we hear it and believe it as God speaking to us.

By abusing our freedom we can turn deaf ears to God. We can tune Him out and refuse to hear the Bible as personal address. In this way we can frustrate its offer of salvation to us— but we cannot frustrate its warning of judgment upon us. Where unbelief persists the Bible does not function as God's message of salvation, *but it then functions as God's word of judgment.* In one way or another, the Bible will be fulfilled. People cannot put the Word of God under their own control by continuing in sin and unbelief.

B. *That God should speak to us at all is a matter of pure grace.*

We do not deserve a message from Him, for we have sinned against Him so often and so terribly. Should He choose to ignore us completely, should He allow us to pursue our foolish way to eternal ruin, that would be simple justice. As Wesley put it, God has "condescended" to show us the way to heaven. *The Bible is material evidence of the love of God for sinners.* To leave the Bible unread, unheard, unbelieved, and unpracticed is both ungrateful and suicidal. We owe it to ourselves to listen as God, in His infinite mercy, speaks to us through the Bible.

14

III. THE BIBLE SPEAKS TO US ABOUT OUR BELIEFS

A. *As God's Word, personally addressed to us, the Bible controls our beliefs.*

The final test of any doctrinal statement is this: Does the Bible teach it? If not, we should not bind our reason and conscience to that doctrinal statement. The Word of God, and not the opinions of men, is authoritative for our faith and life. Without this objective authority, an authority independent of our minds and sovereign over our minds, we would flounder endlessly in a subjective swamp, never able to say, "This is truth."

What I have just written needs slight amendment. The Bible *as we understand it* is God's Word, which controls our beliefs. As God's Word, the Bible speaks clearly and accurately. God's transmitter is perfect. Our receivers, however, are imperfect, and our understanding of Scripture may be sincere but mistaken. We do not correct our misunderstanding, however, by subjecting the Bible to our beliefs. We are corrected by constantly subjecting our understanding to the Bible. We *continue* to read and hear and obey the Word of God, and in this way our knowledge of Scripture expands and our understanding of its truth becomes a stronger and steadier light upon our paths.

When the apostle Paul preached the gospel of Jesus Christ in the synagogue at Beroea, the listening Jews "received the word with all eagerness, examining the scriptures daily to see if these things were so. Many of them therefore believed" (Acts 17:11-12). Paul's message sounded good to them. They wanted to accept it. Before they could, however, they had to convince themselves that his message really squared with the Scriptures. When they were persuaded that it was biblical, they believed.

Luke regarded their attitude as "noble." Here is a beautiful example of the Bible controlling belief.

Some people sniff at the term *beliefs.* They reject all creeds as "man-made," and they boast of having "no creed but Christ." This may sound pious and spiritual, but it is really nonsense. "Sublime nonsense," perhaps—to borrow a phrase from a friend—but still nonsense. Its sublimity does not offset its folly. "My creed is Christ," someone insists. Very well, but *who* is He? *What* has He done? *Why* do you believe in Him? As soon as one begins to answer such simple questions he is involved in creed-making, like it or not.

Creeds are inescapable. They are summary statements of what we believe. We cannot dismiss them, but we must keep them subject to the Bible. In this way the Church can be "always reformed, always reforming." If the creed becomes our final authority, it usurps the place of the Bible, and we are then guilty of sitting in judgment upon God's Word. With the Bible as our final authority we keep the way open to amend and improve our beliefs.

To say, "God's Word as we understand it," does not mean that we place our understanding above the Word of God. It does mean that we shape our understanding by patient and continuous study of God's Word. The Bible above the creed, in order to shape the creed, should be our rule.

In saying this, we are not putting the Bible between Christ and the Church, or between Christ and the Christian, and thus sidestepping His Lordship over us. Jesus Christ has "all authority in heaven and on earth" (Matt. 28:18). *But He exercises His Lordship over our lives by speaking to us through the Bible.* This is *how* He chooses to govern our beliefs and our behavior.

He may speak in other ways, but however He speaks He never contradicts the Bible. Any "voice" or "revelation" that

16

people claim to receive must be tested by the Bible. In ancient Israel, any message that claimed divine origin was to be tested by the *written* Word of God: "To the teaching and to the testimony! Surely for this word which they speak there is no dawn" (Isa. 8:20). The Christian needs to erect the same test when anyone claims to speak for God. The unscriptural doctrines of men bring no sunrise, no light, to our hearts and paths. The word that brings "dawn" is God's Word.

B. *Beliefs controlled by the Bible can never be divorced from behavior.*

A person may parrot an orthodox creed, but if he lives contrary to the moral demands of Scripture, his behavior is actually governed by lies he has swallowed, not by truths God has spoken. He honors God with his lips, but his heart is far from Him (Isa. 29:13), and life flows from the heart (Prov. 4:23). The Word of God must be deposited in the heart if we would keep our lives from sin (Ps. 119:11).

The scribes and Pharisees who opposed Jesus were well versed in Scripture. They could appeal to the law, *as they interpreted it,* to rationalize their antagonism to Him. They did not hesitate to accuse Him of lawbreaking and blasphemy, which (to their minds) justified *scripturally* His execution on the Cross. What we view as slander and murder they would have defended as loyalty to their Bibles!

This has been true, also, in church history. Calling themselves Christians, people have hated, opposed, and persecuted other Christians. When their destructive behavior was challenged, they could furnish chapter-and-verse defenses until blue in their faces.

This, again, is why our understanding of the Bible must continue to be challenged by the Bible itself. Behavior is determined by belief, but belief may be grounded upon an erroneous interpretation of Scriptures. Only as we are willing to ask and allow the Holy Spirit to illuminate what He has inspired will we be saved from sinning against the very Bibles we profess to esteem as authoritative.

God speaks through the Bible to teach, reprove, correct, and educate in righteousness. By listening, believing, and obeying, "the man of God may be complete, equipped for every good work" (2 Tim. 3:17). Christians are called upon to "adorn the doctrine of God our Savior" (Titus 2:10). We are to enflesh in holy lives the teaching of Scripture, not the theories of a world in revolt against its Creator. Our life-styles will reflect our beliefs, and our beliefs should be shaped and controlled by the Word of God.

*　*　*

God speaks. *Are we listening?*

Once Jeremiah was arrested, beaten, and imprisoned because politicians hated his messages. He preached what they needed to hear, not what they wanted to hear. The message of judgment upon sin is never welcomed by sinners who will not repent.

Some time later King Zedekiah sent for the prisoner and asked, "Is there any word from the Lord?" Jeremiah replied, "There is," and promptly delivered another unpopular message (Jer. 37:17).

There is always a word from the Lord. Whatever our times, whatever our needs, there is a word from the Lord for each situation. The critical question is not Has God spoken? but Are we listening?

Too many people, mouthing defiance of truth, drown out

all voices but their own. Then they complain that God is silent. Judgment falls on their unforsaken sins, and they protest that God is unfair. God is neither mute nor unjust. The fault lies with wicked leaders and blind followers who refuse to listen, vainly hoping that the Word of God that they reject will not come true.

Jeremiah supplied the king with a simple alternative to destruction—"Obey the Lord." If sinners repent, God will forgive. If sinners persist in their rebellion, God will destroy. This is just as true for sinners in the house of God as for sinners in the haunts of evil. Sin and die, obey and live—those are the only options.

Zedekiah refused to hear. As a consequence, he was captured by an alien army, compelled to watch the execution of his sons, and then blinded. He languished in prison until his death (Jer. 52:8-11). *There is no escape from the Word of the Lord.*

God has spoken. The Bible is His Word to us. Are we listening? God can shout in our ears until our brains rattle, but unless we obey Him nothing can prevent righteous judgment from overtaking us. If we believe His Word, obey its commands, and claim its promises, we can be victorious in all circumstances.

This, then, is how we should receive and read our Bibles—as the Word of God; as His Word addressed personally to us; and as His Word with authority to determine what we believe and how we behave. The Bible must occupy a place in our lives unshared by all other books, however good those other books may be.

By what God speaks through the Bible we are to test what people say in their speeches and writings. Where they agree with Scripture we can receive their messages thankfully, but always the authority for our doctrines and conduct should be Scripture itself.

Truth at Work:

1. What does it mean to say that the Bible is *God's* Word?

2. What does it mean to say that the Bible is God's Word *in men's words?*

3. Why is it important to listen to the Bible *along with the church* and not simply by oneself?

4. What has the Bible said to *you* recently that *produced a change* in your life?

2

The Bible Speaks of God

God has chosen to make himself known through the Bible.

Of course, we cannot *fully* know Him, not if we read the Bible from cover to cover for years and years. *Only God has the capacity to fully comprehend God.* Often husbands and wives, even after living together for years, discover intriguing elements of mystery in their understanding of each other. It should be no surprise, then, that the being and action of God surpasses the grasp of our minds. When we have learned all we possibly can of God, we will still be compelled to say with an ancient sufferer, "Lo, these are but the outskirts of his ways; and how small a whisper do we hear of him!" (Job 26:14).

Although we cannot fully know God, we can *truly* know Him. The Bible does not mislead us. The knowledge of God that eludes us, because it is so vast, is surely in harmony with the knowledge of God given to us in the Bible. God is *more* than Scripture discloses, but He is not *other* than Scripture reveals. When we face God at the end of our lives, He will not seem alien to us. We will recognize Him from His portrait in the Bible.

In this chapter we will focus upon the major aspects of our relationship to God. The obvious starting place is this:

I. THE BIBLE SPEAKS TO US ABOUT GOD AS CREATOR

A. *Divine creation is clearly and powerfully affirmed in Scripture.*

The Bible does not hesitate or stutter at this point. The very opening words of Scripture declare, "In the beginning God created the heavens and the earth" (Gen. 1:1). These majestic words are too deep for a philosopher to fathom but too clear for a fool to miss.

The universe has not always existed. It did not happen through some accidental interplay of random force and eternal matter. It had a beginning. It was conceived in the mind of God and spoken into existence by the will of God. "God said, 'Let there be' . . . and there was . . ." (v. 3). In the first chapter of Genesis the creative phrase, "And God said," occurs nine times.

The time-space universe was created by the Word of God who is eternal, who is beyond time but within time, who is beyond space but within space. "This is my Father's world," wrote the hymnist, and he never penned a truer line.

Many scientists dismiss the concept of creation with an impatient shrug. Others subject bits and pieces of the world to intense scrutiny, trying to determine when and how creation occurred. But to know *who* created all things they must either turn to the Bible or remain in ignorance.

No one can improve upon the Psalmist's confession of faith: "By the word of the Lord the heavens were made, and all their host by the breath of his mouth. . . . For he spoke, and it came to be; he commanded, and it stood forth" (Ps. 33:6, 9).

The wisdom, power, and love of God constitute the only adequate explanation for our world. It was created by Him, and it is sustained by Him. The earth—our home in this vast universe—was made from nothing and hung upon nothing. As Job exclaimed, "He stretches out the north over the void, and hangs the earth upon nothing" (Job 26:7). The shocks and concussions of passing millennia have not shaken it from that hook! God upholds it.

Scripture does not recognize what we call secondary causes. It attributes both the origin and the upkeep of the world to God. He waters the earth and makes the grasses grow. Bread for man and fodder for beasts are His loving provisions. If He takes away their breath, the creatures die; when He sends forth His Spirit they are created and renewed (Ps. 104:14-15, 27-30).

All things are dependent upon their Maker. He is the ultimate Source of all that sustains us. As James puts it, "Every good endowment and every perfect gift is from above, coming down from the Father" (1:17). In the words of Maltbie Babcock:

> Back of the loaf is the snowy flour,
> And back of the flour the mill,
> And back of the mill is the wheat and the shower,
> And the sun and the Father's will.

B. *The New Testament attributes creation to the Lord Jesus Christ.*

Paul wrote, "All things were created through him and for him. He is before all things, and in him all things hold together" (Col. 1:16-17). John wrote, "In the beginning was the Word, and the Word was with God, and the Word was God. He was in the beginning with God; all things were made through him" (John 1:1-3).

This creative Word "became flesh and dwelt among us" in

Jesus Christ. Think of it! In Jesus Christ the Creator was united with the creature, a mystery that transcends reason and makes possible our salvation. That makes me want to do two things at once—scratch my head in confusion and praise the Lord in gratitude.

Since Christ is the Creator, to be a Christian is to have fellowship with our Maker. Any abuse of creation places a perilous strain upon that fellowship. Christians cannot, in good conscience, ravage or pollute nature. They cannot treat with contempt the handiwork of God. To abuse His art is to insult the Artist. Respect for all creatures should be a hallmark of Christianity.

This does not mean that all creatures are to be treated alike. God deals with every creature according to its nature. He deals with rocks as rocks, with camels as camels, with persons as persons. Creation has a scale of values, and the Creator has placed human beings at the top. Before creating them God paused, held a council, and decreed their making in His "own image" (Gen. 1:26). Man has a capacity for conscious communion with God that sets him above every other creature. To forget this is to demean persons and to dishonor God.

We should not value anything on earth above persons— not forests, rivers, mines, factories, houses, lands, birds, beasts, or anything else. We should never treat persons as things to be exploited for our pleasure or profit. To reduce ourselves or others to the level of animals, even the most sophisticated animals, is degrading to humanity and insulting to God. People are more than animals who learned to walk on their hind legs and read books.

> *A hungry ass will bray,*
> *A starving man find will to pray.*
> *Wolf-mangled sheep will bleat,*

But suff'ring man the Creed repeat.
Hurt bears will vengeance seek,
But injured man forgiveness speak.
Deny it, skeptic, as you can—
There's something vastly more to man!

That "something vastly more" is called in Scripture "the image of God." Sin has defaced that image, but Christ restores it. The Christian cannot scorn those who are the objects of God's love, of Christ's atoning death, and of the Holy Spirit's renewing power.

The Bible teaches that all creation was involved in man's fall from God. And the whole creation will be restored: "According to his promise we wait for new heavens and a new earth in which righteousness dwells" (2 Pet. 3:13). The restoration of nature to its pristine glory awaits the completed redemption of mankind (Rom. 8:18-24). Meanwhile, the convulsions of a groaning nature may produce some calamitous events. The earth over which man was told to exercise dominion will often seem more like a vengeful enemy than a cooperative servant.

The fact that man and his world are "fallen," however, gives us no excuse to mistreat people or their environment. God told the first man to "have dominion" over earth and its creatures (Gen. 1:28). Some have read into these words a human right to impose any treatment upon the earth that man desires. But man is supposed to rule over the earth *as the servant of God.* His stewardship ought to reflect the Creator's purpose and respect for creation. Whenever he ravages and pollutes the resources of nature, man is exercising a satanic dominion. For his rebellion and greed he will surely be judged.

Even in their "fallen" condition, "The heavens are telling

25

the glory of God" (Ps. 19:1) and "the whole earth is full of his glory" (Isa. 6:3). Those whose eyes have been opened by grace behold this glory, and they are inspired to worship. Those who cannot see turn themselves into gods who violate nature or turn nature into gods that enslave mankind. We can only sustain a right relationship to nature and to persons when we have been reconciled to God, their Creator.

This fact brings us to consider a second major element in our relationship to God:

II. THE BIBLE SPEAKS TO US ABOUT GOD AS REDEEMER

Scripture is filled with the language of redemption.

To Israel, God said, "I am the Lord your Savior, and your Redeemer, the Mighty One of Jacob" (Isa. 49:26). God exercised His Lordship and Saviorhood by redeeming His people. This work of redemption is associated with power—it is accomplished by "the Mighty One."

"Jacob" is the name the prophet used for God's people when he wanted to stress their corruption and helplessness. It is their name as a people who have sinned, who are suffering the consequences of their rebellion against God, and who are helpless to effect their own deliverance. Into their desperate predicament God comes in His power, and rescue takes place. God redeems Jacob; God saves sinners.

A. *Redemption requires power.*

Slaves and captives are not easily liberated. "The Mighty One" alone possesses power adequate to gain our release from sin.

> *He breaks the pow'r of canceled sin;*
> *He sets the pris'ner free.*

26

God promised to redeem Israel from Egyptian bondage "with an outstretched arm and with great acts of judgment" (Exod. 6:6). When Pharaoh's army pursued the fleeing slaves, God parted the Sea of Reeds and allowed the fugitives to escape. When the Egyptian warriors plunged into that escape route God closed the parted waters, and the posse was drowned. Free at last, the happy Israelites sang, "Thy right hand, O Lord, glorious in power, thy right hand, O Lord, shatters the enemy" (15:6). The "arm" and "right hand" of God are verbal symbols for His invincible saving power.

In the Old Testament the biggest power display was the Exodus. There God divided the sea, liberated the slaves, and brought judgment on Pharaoh. In the New Testament the biggest power display is the bloody cross and empty tomb of Christ. There God broke the grip of sin and death, freeing all who trust in the risen Lord Jesus Christ.

B. *Redemption involves price.*

The verb *redeem* means literally "to buy back." It refers to the price paid to ransom slaves from bondage or prisoners from captivity. Even millionaire sinners are morally bankrupt. Whatever a man's bank account, he cannot redeem himself or others. The sinless Christ alone could pay that price. *He was the price!* As Peter reminded the church: "You were ransomed . . . not with perishable things such as silver or gold, but with the precious blood of Christ" (1 Pet. 1:18-19).

In his Epistles Peter identifies three things as "precious": (1) the "precious blood" by which Christ atoned for our sins; (2) the "precious promises" by which salvation is offered to us; and (3) the "precious faith" by which we appropriate that blood-bought salvation as our personal experience. The great-

27

est of these three is the precious Blood, the price Jesus paid to free us from our bondage to sin and death.

A century ago Cecil Alexander penned some profoundly simple verses about this blood-redemption that Christians are still singing today:

> *There is a green hill far away,*
> *Without a city wall,*
> *Where the dear Lord was crucified,*
> *Who died to save us all.*
>
> *We may not know, we cannot tell*
> *What pains He had to bear;*
> *But we believe it was for us*
> *He hung and suffered there.*
>
> *He died that we might be forgiv'n,*
> *He died to make us good,*
> *That we might go at last to heav'n,*
> *Saved by His precious blood.*
>
> *There was no other good enough*
> *To pay the price of sin;*
> *He only could unlock the gate*
> *Of heav'n and let us in.*

The scarred slopes of Calvary may not have been green, but the essential truth of the hymn abides. Only Jesus, the spotless Lamb of God, could atone for sin.

Because man is "Jacob," because he is weak and helpless, salvation is offered to him upon simple conditions. He is to repent of his sins and believe on Jesus Christ, the Redeemer. Salvation cannot be purchased by the richest of sinners, but it is not denied to the poorest of them. We are saved "by grace" and "through faith" (Eph. 2:8). That places salvation within the reach of all—rich and poor, learned and ignorant, and all those in between—for God has given grace that enables anyone who hears the gospel to repent and to believe.

C. *Redemption means possession.*

God frees us from sin by binding us to himself. "You are not your own," Paul wrote, "you were bought with a price. So glorify God in your body" (1 Cor. 6:19-20). God does not free us to "do our own thing." That is what caused mankind's trouble in the beginning. Having our own way is the very essence of sin. The law of the redeemed life is the will of God, and the will of God is *holiness.* His people are committed, by the very fact of redemption, to lives of moral purity and integrity (1 Thess. 4:1-8).

This does not mean that one form of bondage is exchanged for another. Doing God's will is our freedom. That is what we are created to do. That is what it means to be truly human. Having our own way is slavery, a lesson that people learn only with difficulty.

The prodigal son left home in quest of freedom, fortune, and fun. He ended up miserable, bankrupt, and enslaved. Only by submitting himself to the father's will did he find what he had been seeking in vain.

Outside the will of God we have no more freedom than a derailed locomotive or a beached whale. We were designed to operate in one element—the will of God. Out of that element we break down and perish.

Jesus said, "Every one who commits sin is a slave to sin. . . . if the Son makes you free, you will be free indeed" (John 8:34, 36). God is no despot. In the will of Him who is love we experience the most glorious freedom to be found in this world and in the world to come.

Charles Kingsley said, "There are two freedoms—the false, where a man is free to do what he likes; the true, where a man is free to do what he ought." But the fully redeemed person discovers that the will of God is both duty and pleasure. He can say with the Psalmist, "I *delight* to do thy will, O my God; thy law is within my heart" (Ps. 40:8, italics added).

Because the will of God is the responsibility of the redeemed, there is another vital relationship that God bears to us.

III. THE BIBLE SPEAKS TO US ABOUT GOD AS JUDGE

A. *Judgment is an inescapable event.*

We are accountable unto God. He is Lord and we are stewards. Accountability is integral to stewardship.

When Adam and Eve sinned they were confronted by God, who asked, "What is this that you have done?" (Gen. 3:13). Paul warns us that we shall experience the same confrontation in the future: "We shall all stand before the judgment seat of God." On that solemn occasion "each of us shall give account of himself to God" (Rom. 14:10, 12). There is no escape from this reckoning, because accountability is an essential element of humanity. Part of what it means to be a creature is to answer to the Creator for one's life.

God has "fixed a day on which he will judge the world in righteousness." He has appointed Jesus Christ to execute that judgment (Acts 17:31; see also John 5:22-29). That Judge cannot be deceived or bribed, and from His sentence there can be no appeal.

30

B. *Judgment has a moral accent.*

In the Old Testament a judge was not primarily one who presided over lawsuits but one who championed the oppressed and restored a right order in society. The judge delivered his people and punished his enemies, often marching at the head of an army recruited to strike a blow for freedom: "Then the Lord raised up judges, who saved them out of the power of those who plundered them" (Judg. 2:16). Legal functions were secondary to their careers.

In their preaching of judgment, however, the prophets emphasized the *moral* factor. They proclaimed a coming "day of the Lord" when judgment would be visited upon the sins of all nations, even the sins of the covenant people (Amos 5:18-24; Joel 1:13-15).

The New Testament identifies the "day of the Lord" with the return of Jesus Christ (2 Peter 3). Final judgment has been committed to Him, and before Him all nations and all persons will appear (Matt. 25:31-32; Rev. 20:12). His coming in glory will bring about the ultimate vindication of His followers and destruction of His foes. Paul describes this event of judgment in awesome words:

> *God deems it just to repay with affliction those who afflict you, and to grant rest with us to you who are afflicted, when the Lord Jesus is revealed from heaven with his mighty angels in flaming fire, inflicting vengeance upon those who do not know God and upon those who do not obey the gospel of our Lord Jesus. They shall suffer the punishment of eternal destruction and exclusion from the presence of the Lord and from the glory of his might, when he comes on that day to be glorified in his saints, and to be marveled at in all who have believed* (2 Thess. 1:6-10).

31

C. *Judgment is a neglected truth.*

Little is preached today about judgment, but we are fools to ignore it. God is "the Judge of all the earth" (Gen. 18:25), and human history has its terminus at His judgment seat. "It is appointed for men to die once, and after that comes judgment" (Heb. 9:27). Every passing moment brings us closer to that appointment, one we did not make and cannot break.

Because God is our Judge we are forbidden to judge one another (Matt. 7:1-2; Rom. 14:13). We are not to stand against others in judgment but with others under judgment. This does not mean that we should neither oppose sin nor administer discipline within the church. Condemnation is forbidden, but discrimination must be practiced (Matt. 7:6, 15-20; 1 Cor. 5:1—6:6).

When we trust in Christ to save us, we are "justified by faith." A sentence of acquittal is passed upon us; we are released from our guilt; and we thus escape the wrath of God that is coming upon the unrighteous. The truth of coming judgment is a call to repent of our sins and believe in the Lord Jesus Christ "who delivers us from the wrath to come" (1 Thess. 1:10).

* * *

Jesus taught us that God's best name is "Father," a name that pardoned sinners dare to use with intimacy when they commune with God in prayer.

He is the Father-Creator; He is the Father-Redeemer; He is the Father-Judge. Underlying all His activities and undergirding all our hopes is this greatest of truths—"God is love" (1 John 4:16). This is the God of whom the Bible speaks to us.

32

Truth at Work:

1. What is the significance of the doctrine of creation for *interpersonal relationships?*

2. Why is our rescue from sin and death couched so frequently in the *terminology of redemption* in Scripture?

3. What are some implications of the intensely *personal* nature of final judgment?

4. Are you allowing in *your* heart and life any attitudes or actions you are unwilling to face *in the judgment?*

3

The Bible Speaks of Jesus Christ

The primary purpose of the Bible is to tell us about Jesus Christ. As Peter said to the household of Cornelius, "To him all the prophets bear witness" (Acts 10:43).

Apart from the Bible we could not learn about Him. The secular records that date from "the days of his flesh" (Heb. 5:7) contain a couple of ambiguous references to Him—that is all. To ancient historians He was not important. How quickly their poor judgment was condemned! Jesus has greater significance for human life than all other persons who ever lived—put together.

While secular annals are silent, the Bible centers on Jesus Christ. Old Testament writers foretold His coming into the world. New Testament writers announced that coming and interpreted the meaning of His life, death, and resurrection. These events are viewed as "the mighty works of God" (Acts 2:11) by which we are saved from sin and death.

Only the Bible tells us about Jesus, and it tells us only what we need to know of Him. It leaves unanswered hundreds of questions about Him that occur to our inquisitive minds. His growing-up years, for example, are veiled from us. Scholars call them "the hidden years at Nazareth." The witness of Scripture to Christ concentrates on the three brief years of public ministry that culminated in His death on the Cross.

What Scripture affirms of Christ is brief but sufficient for our salvation. It identifies His *person* and interprets His *mission*.

I. THE BIBLE TELLS US WHO JESUS IS

A. *He is the Son of God.*

How simple that is to say; how difficult to explain! The bottom line is this—Jesus stands in a relationship to God that is unshared and unsharable by all other humans and even by the angels.

Angels are called "sons of God" in the Bible (Ps. 29:1; 89:6, margins) but never in the sense that Jesus is called the Son of God. Men, too, are called the sons of God in the Bible (Gal. 3:26; 4:6) but never in the sense that Jesus is called the Son of God.

The Letter to the Hebrews declares Him to be "as much superior to angels as the name he has obtained is more excellent than theirs" (1:4). He is the "first-born" whose entrance "into the world" was accompanied by the command, "Let all God's angels worship him" (1:6).

John the Revelator fell down before an angel to worship and was rebuked. The angel said, "You must not do that! I am a fellow servant with you and your brethren the prophets, and with those who keep the words of this book. Worship God" (Rev. 22:8-9).

Cornelius, a Roman army officer, "fell down at [Peter's] feet and worshiped him" (Acts 10:25). The horrified apostle reached down and lifted the soldier to his feet, saying, "Stand up; I too am a man" (v. 26).

When superstitious pagans tried to worship Paul and Barnabas, these apostles "tore their garments" (Acts 14:14) in emotional anguish, crying out, "Men, why are you doing this? We also are men . . ." They were not gods but messengers of "a living God who made the heaven and the earth and the sea and all that is in them" (v. 15). They had come, they insisted, to preach "good news" that calls for the renunciation of idols.

Worshiping angels or men is expressly forbidden, yet *both angels and men are commanded to worship Jesus Christ.* Nothing could make clearer the truth that Jesus stands in a unique relationship to God.

Jesus himself was certainly conscious of this unique relationship to God. He taught His disciples, when they prayed, to say *"Our* Father" (Matt. 6:9; Luke 11:2), for they all bore the same relationship to God. Each was a son of God in the identical sense that the others were sons of God. But when He included himself with the disciples, Jesus used the phrases "my Father and your Father" and "my God and your God" (John 20:17). He knew that He was the Son of God in a sense that they were not.

Jesus was truly and fully human, but He was also truly and fully divine. As the Son of God, He existed "before the world was made" (John 17:5). Indeed, He existed as the world's Maker! In simple words with bottomless meanings John opens his Gospel with this statement:

> *In the beginning was the Word, and the Word was with God, and the Word was God. He was in the beginning with God; all things were made through him, and without him was not anything made that was made. . . .*
>
> *And the Word became flesh and dwelt among us, full of grace and truth; we have beheld his glory, glory as of the only Son from the Father* (1:1-3, 14).

The Creator became a creature. The eternal entered into history. God became a man. Awesome!

He was so human that He could sleep in a tossing boat, exhausted from His labors of love. Yet, awakened by His terrified disciples, He could silence the screaming winds and calm the raging waves with a word of command: "Peace! Be still!" "A great storm" at once became "a great calm" (Mark 4:37, 39).

Does that "blow your mind"? Good. The human mind is highly efficient but decidedly limited. In any area of investigation, from stars to worms, "we know in part." We do not understand one another. That Jesus Christ, the Son of God, is beyond our comprehension should be our comfort, not our frustration. A Christ we could figure out, a Christ no larger than a mirror image of even the greatest men, could not rescue us from sin and reconcile us to God.

B. *Jesus is the Son of man.*

This was His favorite self-designation. And it was more than a way of saying, as the Divine One, "I am also human." It was that, but much more than that.

The title "Son of man" has its roots in Jesus' own Bible, the Old Testament, with which He was well acquainted. There the expression is used in three ways.

First, it designates man—the human creature. The Psalmist asks, "What is man that thou art mindful of him, and the son of man that thou dost care for him?" (Ps. 8:4). This is an example of what is called Hebrew parallelism, where a word in one line is given a synonym in the following line. "Man" and "son of man" are synonymous.

Second, "Son of man" is used as a designation for Ezekiel the prophet. This is how God customarily addressed him. The first occurrence is found in 2:1, where God says, "Son of man, stand upon your feet, and I will speak with you." The phrase is similarly used 90 more times. Here, then, it designates a human creature called and commissioned to bear the message of God to his contemporaries.

Third, "Son of man" occurs in a recorded vision of Daniel. The prophet beheld "one like a son of man" who came before "the Ancient of Days" and received from Him "an everlasting dominion" (7:13-14). This "son of man" is a heavenly figure who receives from God an indestructible and eternal kingdom, which He shares with "the people of the saints of the Most High" (v. 27).

Scholars are convinced that the reference to this heavenly ruler is most decisive for our understanding of Jesus Christ as the "Son of man." All of the Old Testament usages can apply, however. Jesus is a man; Jesus is a prophet; and Jesus is a ruler whom the Father has chosen, anointed, and destined to occupy a throne and reign over His people forever.

The angel Gabriel, when telling the virgin Mary that she would mother the Messiah, said,

> Behold, you will conceive in your womb and bear a son, and you shall call his name Jesus. He will be great, and will be called the Son of the Most High; and the Lord God will give to him the throne of his father David, and he will reign over the house of Jacob for ever; and of his kingdom there will be no end. . . . the child to be born will be called holy, the Son of God (Luke 1:31-33, 35).

See how the divine and human factors coalesce in this Annunciation. The human name is there—"Jesus"—meaning Savior. The divine title is there—"the Son of God"—both revealing and concealing mysteries of His person and mission.

And there, also, is the ruler's task that He will assume as the Son of man—"of his kingdom there will be no end."

C. *Jesus is Lord.*

When we move from the Gospels to the Epistles another title dominates. There Jesus is not as frequently called "Son" or "Son of God" or "Son of man," but most often He is called "Lord."

"Lord" is a title that bears witness also to a man who is more than man, who is divine. When the Old Testament was translated into Greek, the name of God—*Yahweh*—was rendered as *Kyrios*—"Lord." In the New Testament, the apostles give this divine title regularly to Jesus.

Those apostles were reared in the strict tradition of Jewish monotheism. Daily they recited the ancient creed: "Hear, O Israel: The Lord our God is one Lord" (Deut. 6:4). That those very apostles adopted as their earliest creed, "Jesus is Lord," makes it impossible to subtract divinity from the title.

It was this Lordship of Jesus, a Lordship *experienced* by the Church, which compelled early Christian thinkers to formulate the doctrine of the Trinity. The grace of God by which they were saved from sin was "the grace of the Lord Jesus" (1 Cor. 16:23). *They gave the name of God to a man and offered joyfully to that man the worship that belongs only to God.* The alternative is inescapable: *Either Jesus is the God-man or Christianity is idolatry.*

The apostles did not originate the ascription of Lordship to Christ. Jesus referred to himself in this way, combining the deepest humility with the loftiest title. When He had bathed the feet of His disciples He said, "You call me Teacher and Lord; and you are right, for so I am. If I then, your Lord and

Teacher, have washed your feet, you also ought to wash one another's feet" (John 13:13-14).

The risen Christ stood before His followers and said, "All authority in heaven and on earth has been given to me" (Matt. 28:18). From that moment, those disciples adopted as their irreducible creed, "Jesus is Lord of all." Rather than compromise that faith, or yield that title even to Caesar, they went to prison and to death.

"The man Christ Jesus" is *truly* human, but He is not *merely* human. He is the God-man, however impossible that sounds to human reason, however difficult that is to grasp or explain intellectually.

II. THE BIBLE TELLS US WHAT JESUS DOES

We have glanced at titles that inform us concerning the person of Christ. There are other titles that summarize His mission. They are found throughout the New Testament, but a convenient cluster of them occurs in the opening chapter of John's Gospel.

The Gospel of John emphasizes the ministry of Jesus as a mission. Over 40 times He is designated as the One "sent" into the world by the Father to speak the Father's words and do the Father's works (e.g., 7:16; 12:48-50).

His mission is introduced by John the Baptist. John the Baptist himself appears as "a man sent from God" (1:6) to bear witness to Jesus Christ. In the testimony John bears there are three titles that stand out with special significance—"the light," "the Lamb," and "the Lord."

A. *To call Jesus "the light" means that* **He reveals God to us.**

He is "the true light that enlightens every man" (v. 9). From the dawn of history, mankind has been haunted by the

40

question, "What is God like?" When Moses cried out to God, "Show me thy glory" (Exod. 33:18), he articulated humanity's deepest longing. The answer to that cry was given in Jesus Christ. "No one has ever seen God; the only Son, who is in the bosom of the Father, *he has made him known*" (John 1:18, italics added). In the earthly life of Jesus, God made himself known as fully and truly as possible. In Jesus Christ, the invisible God became visible.

When the ministry of Jesus was nearing its close, one of the disciples exclaimed, "Lord, show us the Father, and we shall be satisfied." Jesus' reply was, "He who has seen me has seen the Father" (John 14:8-9). God was revealed in Christ.

Paul affirms this same truth. He wrote, "For it is the God who said, 'Let light shine out of darkness,' who has shone in our hearts to give the light of the knowledge of the glory of God *in the face of Christ*" (2 Cor. 4:6).

The words and the deeds of Jesus—as He acted, reacted, and interacted with all kinds of people in all kinds of situations—are our transcripts of the mind and heart of God. The love, mercy, wisdom, justice, holiness, and wrath of God are spelled out in the life and death of Jesus Christ. To know what God is like, read the Gospels and look at Jesus. He is "the light."

That light will make clear our pathway out of sin unto God. It will lead us unerringly and invincibly as we follow its guidance. "The light shines in the darkness, and the darkness has not overcome it" (John 1:5). "I am the light of the world," said Jesus; "he who follows me will not walk in darkness, but will have the light of life" (8:12). Apart from Him there is only spiritual darkness leading to eternal darkness.

B. *To call Jesus "the Lamb" means that **He redeems us from sin.***

As Jesus approached him one day, John the Baptist exclaimed, "Behold, the Lamb of God, who takes away the sin of the world!" (John 1:29).

The background of this title is rich and varied. Recall the story of the Exodus. Lambs were slain and their blood was applied to the door frames of Israel's homes when God rescued them from slavery. Each year lambs were slain when that redemption was commemorated at the Passover feast. Lambs were slain morning and evening each day at the Temple altar. And in Isaiah 53 a man is described as a lamb who bears the sins of all his people in atoning death. These various sacrifices anticipated the coming of Christ. He is the Lamb of God, the redemptive Sacrifice that purchased our acceptance with God and deliverance from sin.

Only human life has the value of human life. No animal sacrifice could redeem persons. No sinful human life could redeem sinners. Only the spotless Lamb of God, who "bore our sins in his body on the tree" (1 Pet. 2:24), could provide the stripes by which we are healed.

Jesus is "the Lamb." As the apostle Paul expressed it, "Christ, our paschal lamb, has been sacrificed" for us (1 Cor. 5:7). And Peter reminds us that we are ransomed from sin "with the precious blood of Christ, like that of a lamb without blemish or spot" (1 Pet. 1:19). Every lamb sacrificed in Israel pointed forward to the time when Christ "offered himself without blemish to God" (Heb. 9:11) to "bear the sins of many" (v. 28) once for all (see vv. 11-28).

The heart of the Bible is its frequent insistence upon the death of Jesus Christ as an atonement for our sins. "Without the shedding of blood," God has decreed, "there is no forgiveness of sins" (Heb. 9:22). The gates of eternal life are hinged upon the cross of Jesus Christ. As Robert Lowry taught the church to sing,

> *What can wash away my sin?*
> *Nothing but the blood of Jesus.*
> *What can make me whole again?*
> *Nothing but the blood of Jesus.*

> *For my pardon this I see—*
> *Nothing but the blood of Jesus.*
> *For my cleansing this my plea—*
> *Nothing but the blood of Jesus.*

C. *To call Jesus "the Lord" means that* **He rules us in love.**

John the Baptist cried, "Make straight the way of the Lord" (John 1:23). When Jesus comes to our hearts as Savior, He comes also as Lord. He will not share the throne of our hearts with others, not even with us. He must be first—before self, before family, before country, before church. We can be His disciples only as we submit to His Lordship. When He frees us from sin, He takes us captive to the will of God.

But that captivity is our true liberty. The rule of Christ is our only freedom. If we are dominated by ourselves or by others, the result is bondage and misery. The very essence of sin is self-will, rebellion against God. The essence of freedom is obedience to His will, for we are created to live in the will of the Lord, and only there can we be fulfilled as human persons.

His banner over us is love! He is no despot. He rules in perfect love, wisdom, and justice. He is committed to our highest welfare, a commitment He has signed in the blood of His cross. To serve Jesus Christ is not submission to tyranny; it is the discovery of a liberating love.

43

In fulfilling His mission, Jesus focused His love and power upon the individual. To Him, everyone mattered—"the last, the least, and the lost." He looked for those whom the world overlooked. He befriended those who were friendless. He helped those who were helpless. This also is borne out emphatically in John's Gospel, though it shines through the other Gospels as well.

Jesus made the first clear announcement of His Messiahship, not to the religious leaders of His own community, but to a five-time loser at marriage who was now living in adultery. When this Samaritan woman said, "Messiah is coming," Jesus replied, "I who speak to you am he" (John 4:25, 26). Others scorned her, but Jesus offered her a spring of living water—eternal life.

In the five porches at Bethesda were "a multitude of invalids" (John 5:3). "One man was there" (v. 5) who had been helplessly ill for 38 years. "Jesus saw him"! (v. 6). He never overlooks the individual within the crowd. No one is faceless and nameless to Him. The man was helpless, friendless, and penniless—but Jesus loved, sought, and healed him.

Similar incidents abound in the Gospels, and they have been multiplied by thousands throughout history. Jesus is building a church, a family, a people, but He does so by bringing the redeeming benefits of His love to individuals. This truth is of special importance to our generation, when so often the structures and forces of society depersonalize and dehumanize. We are not just numbers in ledgers or data in computers. We are persons for whom Christ died and to whom He offers salvation.

Each of us matters to Jesus Christ! That being true, we should matter to ourselves, and we should matter to one another. We cannot follow Christ and treat ourselves or others with contempt. We cannot live like nobodies or regard others as nobodies. The Bible calls upon us to love our neighbors as ourselves and to esteem others highly. Jesus demands and enables us to act toward everyone as He did.

*   *   *

Jesus Christ is the focus of the Bible's witness. He is the divine-human One whose person and mission are alike unique. He alone discloses God to mankind, reconciles mankind to God, and governs the redeemed as God with absolute authority and quenchless love. Through the Bible to Christ is the grandest journey anyone ever makes!

Truth at Work:

1. Why should we *worship* Jesus Christ?

2. What happens when the Saviorhood and Lordship of Jesus are *separated?*

3. If animal life cannot atone for human life, why was a system of *animal sacrifices* instituted?

4. How has the power of Jesus Christ to *save from sin* been demonstrated in your life?

4

The Bible Speaks of the Holy Spirit

The Holy Spirit has been called "the executive of the Godhead." I forget where I first read that, but it's true. He carries into effect what the Father has purposed from eternity and what the Son has provided in history.

The dominant quality of the Holy Spirit is power. Power is constantly associated with Him throughout the Bible. He is the power of God at the point where human life is touched and changed by divine grace. Through the Spirit's power, the Father's will to save us, and the Son's work to redeem us become ours in actual, personal experience.

While the Holy Spirit is associated with power, the Holy Spirit is not merely an influence or a power. He is a person.

I was riding home from court once with a lawyer. He was a church leader and wanted to talk theology. Somehow we got on the subject of the Holy Spirit. He said, "I conceive of the Holy Spirit as a benign influence." Waving toward the setting sun, he continued, "Just as the rays of the sun bring light and warmth to the earth, so the Holy Spirit brings spiritual illumination and comfort to our lives."

The Spirit does influence, to be sure, but He is more than an influence, however benign. He empowers, but He is more than a power. We can *grieve* the Spirit (Eph. 4:30), *lie to* the Spirit (Acts 5:3), *blaspheme* the Spirit (Matt. 12:31), and *quench* the Spirit (1 Thess. 5:19). The Spirit *speaks* (Acts 10:19), *appoints* (13:2), *forbids* (16:6), *comforts* (9:31), *witnesses* (5:32), *guides* (Gal. 5:18), and *teaches* (1 Cor. 2:13). In short, He receives personal treatment and performs personal functions. He is not an impersonal force; He is the "third person" of the Triune Godhead, one with the Father and the Son. Where He is, therefore, they are said to be also (John 14:23).

Admittedly, "Spirit" is an elusive concept. We find it difficult to define and explain what is meant by "Spirit." I once asked a college class of religion majors to do some free-association—to give me the first word that popped into their minds when I said "Spirit." Their chief responses were "ghost," "spook," "pale blur," etc. More refined terms were given by a few, such as "energy," "influence," "life force," and "enthusiasm." A few, who had taken a bit of theology, blurted out "sanctifier."

There is a passage in John's Gospel that can help us greatly in our effort to understand the Holy Spirit. Jesus promised His disciples, who were troubled by the thought of His leaving, "I will pray the Father, and he will give you *another Counselor,* to be with you for ever" (14:16, italics added).

Another Counselor suggests that the Holy Spirit is the alter ego (other self) of Jesus. Jesus had been their Counselor, their Advocate. He stood beside them, giving them peace, strength, and guidance in the complexities and confusions of life. Now the Holy Spirit would continue this same role, not as a visible person beside them but as an invisible person and power within them.

"Another Counselor" means that the Holy Spirit does not come to us as compensation for the absence of Jesus. Instead,

He is our Lord's way of being always present with His people. The disciples did not "lose" Christ and "gain" the Spirit. The Spirit is the fulfillment of Christ's promise, "Lo, I am with you always, to the close of the age" (Matt. 28:20). As Paul wrote, "The Lord is the Spirit" (2 Cor. 3:17).

In this slim book we cannot possibly examine the total message of the Bible relating to the Holy Spirit, but we will glance at His connection with the major works of God.

I. THE HOLY SPIRIT AND CREATION

A. *The Bible associates the Holy Spirit with creation.*

"In the beginning," when earth was a *chaos*—dark, empty, and formless—"the Spirit of God was moving over the face of the waters" (Gen. 1:1-2). The activity of the Spirit transformed chaos to *cosmos*—to ordered beauty.

The Holy Spirit is the eternal antagonist of chaos, of disorder, of all the distortion, perversion, and corruption wrought by sin. He opposes all that spoils the Creator's intention for His handiwork. In nature and in grace, therefore, He is the great reviver and restorer of creation.

Creation has been marred by sin. The fall of man involved also his natural environment. According to Paul, "the creation was subjected to futility." Ultimately, all creation "will be set free from its bondage to decay and obtain the glorious liberty of the children of God."

Atop one of our headquarters buildings is a large revolving globe. As it rotates, wind pressure causes it to make groaning sounds. Each time I see and hear it, I recall Paul's words, "The whole creation [groans] in travail," awaiting its completed redemption (Rom. 8:23).

Because creation is fallen—disordered and enslaved—the work of the Spirit often takes the form of judgment. In this context "judgment" refers to the restoration and establishment of a right social order—one that allows people to live in greater harmony with one another and with their environment. Through the Spirit's work we can enjoy in larger measure the fruits of freedom, industry, and righteousness.

This concept of judgment is seen most clearly in the book called Judges. This book describes a period in Israel's history, prior to the monarchy, when "every man did what was right in his own eyes" (21:25). The laws of God were not enforced. The people were guilty of twin evils—forgetting the Lord their God, and serving the Baals (2:11-13). As a result, the people of Israel became the prey of neighboring nations who conquered, pillaged, and ruled them. When the Israelites repented and cried to God for mercy, He "raised up judges, who saved them out of the power of those who plundered them" (2:16).

Several times we read that "the Spirit of the Lord" came upon these judges (3:10; 6:34; 11:29; 14:6, 19). This explains the power and success of the judges who smashed Israel's foes and restored Israel's freedom. Some of those judges were not conspicuous for either courage or morality, but the Letter to the Hebrews identifies them as men of faith (11:32-34). Faith allowed them to achieve that for which the Holy Spirit empowered them.

B. *The Bible associates the Holy Spirit with the "new creation" also.*

Israel expected an "age to come," a new creation that would be inaugurated by the Messiah. The outstanding feature of this new creation would be an outpouring of the Holy Spirit upon all God's people.

The New Testament teaches that Jesus is the long-expected Messiah. With His resurrection the new creation has begun. At Pentecost the risen Christ received from the Father, and poured out upon the church, the gift of the Holy Spirit (Acts 2:32-33). Upon men and women, old and young, masters and servants, that gift was bestowed (Acts 2:17-18). Moses once exclaimed, "Would that all the Lord's people were prophets, that the Lord would put his spirit upon them!" (Num. 11:29). His fervent wish was dramatically fulfilled after centuries had passed. On the epochal Day of Pentecost, "They were all filled with the Holy Spirit and began to speak in other tongues, as the Spirit gave them utterance" (Acts 2:4).

This new creation has only begun. The new age has dawned, but sunrise has not given place to high noon. The completion of redemption awaits the return of Christ. We are living in "the overlapping" of the old age and the new age. This is why Paul wrote to the Ephesians,

> *In him you also, who have heard the word of truth, the gospel of your salvation, and have believed in him, were sealed with the promised Holy Spirit, which is the guarantee of our inheritance until we acquire possession of it, to the praise of his glory* (1:13-14).

"Guarantee" translates a Greek word *(arrabon)* that carries the sense of "down payment." We put money down to assure the completion of a purchase. God assures us of our heavenly inheritance, assures us that we will be glorified at last, by filling us with the Holy Spirit. He is not only our greatest present treasure but also the pledge of an inconceivably glorious future. He is "Christ in you, the hope of glory" (Col. 1:27).

II. THE HOLY SPIRIT AND REDEMPTION

The provision of Jesus Christ to redeem us from sin is executed by the Holy Spirit. In the "Paraclete" passages of John's Gospel, this ministry of the Spirit is helpfully summarized.

The Greek word *paraclete* means one called to stand beside, and act on behalf of, another. It has been variously translated "Comforter," "Counselor," "Advocate," and simply "Helper."

A. *As our Counselor, the Holy Spirit **guides**.*

Jesus promised, "He will guide you into all the truth" (John 16:13). To borrow a question from troubled Pilate, "What is truth?" (18:38). Two special answers emerge from Scripture.

Praying to the Father, Jesus said, "Thy word is truth" (John 17:17). The mission of the Holy Spirit is closely connected with the Bible. The "Spirit of truth" inspired the writing of Scripture. The promise of Jesus, cited above, had its primary fulfillment in the creation of the New Testament. Now the Spirit who inspired the writing of the Bible must illumine our study of those writings. Otherwise, we cannot grasp their meaning. The Spirit functions in and with and through the written Word of God to guide our lives.

Jesus also said, "I am . . . the truth" (John 14:6). As the God-man, the Word made flesh, He is the truth about God, about man, and about the essential right relationship between God and man.

In Jesus Christ, God is revealed. "He who has seen me," said Jesus, "has seen the Father" (John 14:9). In Jesus Christ, true humanity is disclosed also. He is "the second man" and "the last Adam" (1 Cor. 15:47, 45).

A college student asked me, "How can you say that Jesus is truly and fully human if He never sinned and never carried the guilt that is every person's burden?" I answered, "Jesus *only* was truly and fully human precisely because 'He committed no sin.' Sin is *accidental* to humanity, not *essential* to it. Because we have sinned we are *less* than fully human. We are defects. Only the Christ, 'who in every respect has been tempted as we are, yet without sin' (Heb. 4:15), has experienced humanity completely."

Jesus is not to be measured by us. We are to be measured by Him. So measured, we must confess with Paul, "All have sinned and fall short of the glory of God" (Rom. 3:23).

The "Spirit of truth" guides us "into all truth" by making known the Christ to whom Scripture bears witness (John 16:13). In doing so, He makes us aware of our sin, makes us hungry to be like Jesus, and makes us realize that only Jesus can remedy our sins and establish the truth in our hearts as the governing principle of our lives.

B. *As our Counselor, the Holy Spirit **convicts.***

Jesus declared,

> *He will convince the world concerning sin and righteousness and judgment: concerning sin, because they do not believe in me; concerning righteousness, because I go to the Father, and you will see me no more; concerning judgment, because the ruler of this world is judged* (John 16:8-11).

Let's look at those statements in their reverse order.

"Of judgment": The Holy Spirit, through the Word of God, makes people aware of the doom of evil. Evil has been "judged" in the cross of Christ, for there the power of Satan was broken (John 12:31-32).

"Of righteousness": The Spirit convinces people that the atoning death of Christ is God's one and only way of freeing the slaves of sin and setting them in a right relationship with himself (Rom. 3:20-26).

"Of sin": The Spirit thus reduces the sin question to "the Son question" and shows us that human destiny hinges on belief or disbelief in Jesus Christ. He sets Christ before us as the touchstone of destiny, as the difference between life and death, between heaven and hell (John 3:36).

I was once summoned to the bedside of a man who had become suddenly and desperately sick. When I asked, "What's the matter?" he replied, "Conviction. Your preaching has me under awful conviction. God has shown me my sins and my need of Christ. But I repressed it. I fought against it, and this has made me sick. That's why I sent for you and not a doctor." We prayed, he believed in Christ, and forgiveness brought healing.

Like those who heard Peter's message at Pentecost, he had been "cut to the heart" (Acts 2:37). I could never have produced such conviction, nor can any preacher. It is the work of the Holy Spirit.

C. *As our Counselor, the Holy Spirit also **pleads**.*

This is the essential work of an advocate—to stand beside and plead the cause of another. W. E. Sangster, in a choice sermon on the subject, has shown that the Spirit pleads in us, for us, and through us.

When we are tempted to sin, the Spirit pleads in us to resist evil and do good. Apart from His strong pleas for righteousness we would constantly dishonor Christ and damage ourselves.

When infirmity and ignorance hinder our prayers, the Spirit pleads for us. He "intercedes for us with sighs too deep for words" (Rom. 8:26).

When we address the lost with the message of the gospel, the Spirit pleads through us, convicting them of sin and attracting them to Christ.

D. *By the power of the Holy Spirit we are* **made new.**

Jesus said, "You must be born anew" (John 3:7). These words were not addressed to a wino, or a thug, or a venal politician. They shocked the ears of a man we would regard as a model citizen. Nicodemus was respectable and religious. He said his prayers, read his Bible, paid his tithes, attended worship services faithfully, and served on the city council. He was a pillar in the community.

Spiritually, however, he was empty and dead. He had not discovered eternal life. Driven by frustration and hunger, he sought out Jesus and was told that rebirth was the answer to his need.

Twice Nicodemus raised the plaintive question, "How?"

Jesus answered the first "how" with reference to the Spirit's quickening ministry. "The wind blows where it wills, and you hear the sound of it, but you do not know whence it comes or whither it goes; so it is with every one who is born of the Spirit" (v. 8). The Holy Spirit, as elusive in His movements and as powerful in His effects as the wind, is the force by which an old man—or any sinner of any age—can have new life.

Jesus answered the second "how" by speaking of His coming death on the Cross. "As Moses lifted up the serpent in the wilderness, so must the Son of man be lifted up, that whoever believes in him may have eternal life" (vv. 14-15). With the story of the bronze serpent (Num. 21:6-9), Nicodemus was familiar. Poisoned Israelites were spared from physical death by looking in obedient faith to that bronze serpent—a strange cure but an effective one! Likewise, we receive spiritual life by trusting in the merit and power of the atoning death of Jesus. On the Cross He bore our sins (1 Pet. 2:24), purchased our pardon (Eph. 1:7), and became our life (Col. 3:4).

The Holy Spirit quickens those who believe in Jesus. They are not merely repaired and repainted but also they are regenerated. They become a "new creation" in Christ (2 Cor. 5:17).

E. *By the power of the Holy Spirit we are **made holy.***

Jesus died not only for our wrongdoing but also for our wrongbeing. His death provided not only our forgiveness for sins committed but also our cleansing from sin inherited from the fall of Adam. "Jesus also suffered outside the gate in order to sanctify the people through his own blood" (Heb. 13:12).

To sanctify means to set apart for God. This is more than a legal arrangement; it is a profound spiritual and moral change. To be utterly devoted to God is to be utterly divorced from sin. "You who love the Lord hate evil" (Ps. 97:10, margin). To love God and hate sin with all our hearts demands a deep inward cleansing. This purging is wrought by the power of the Holy Spirit. Paul wrote,

> *This is the will of God, your sanctification: that you abstain from unchastity ... For God has not called us for uncleanness, but in holiness. Therefore whoever disregards this, disregards not man but God, who gives his Holy Spirit to you* (1 Thess. 4:3, 7-8).

In the gift of the Spirit lies the power to make and keep us holy.

F. *By the power of the Holy Spirit we are **made many.***

Christians are expected to reproduce themselves. The family of God is to be a growing household. To His disciples

55

the risen Christ said, "Go . . . and make disciples of all nations" (Matt. 28:19). Just prior to His ascension He promised, "You shall receive power when the Holy Spirit has come upon you; and you shall be my witnesses . . . to the end of the earth" (Acts 1:8). The Church expands through witnessing to Christ in the power of the indwelling Spirit.

Earlier Jesus had said, "He [the Spirit of truth] will bear witness to me" (John 15:26). Now He says, "You shall be my witnesses." These are not two independent and parallel witnesses. The Holy Spirit witnesses *through the Church* as the Church stands, serves, and speaks for Christ. The Spirit indwells us; He loves through us, reaches out through us, and speaks through us. This is why the apostle Paul could write, "We are ambassadors for Christ, *God making his appeal through us*" (2 Cor. 5:20, italics added).

The Early Church prayed for boldness to speak the Word of God in the face of death threats. God answered by filling them with the Holy Spirit (Acts 4:29-31). As a result, "the word of God increased; and the number of the disciples multiplied greatly" (6:7). *A Spirit-filled church, bearing joyful witness to Christ, will keep a growing edge.*

A friend of mine, dying with cancer, witnessed quietly and earnestly to a doctor who was checking her medical charts. To him the message was strange, and he thought she was delirious. Turning to her brother-in-law who was seated nearby, he asked, "How long has she been like this?" Through tears the brother-in-law responded, "As long as I've known her."

This is how the Lord's people should live and die—as faithful witnesses to His love and power to save from sin. The Holy Spirit prompts that witness and makes it effective for reaching people who need the Savior.

*   *   *

The Holy Spirit is the presence and power of the Lord with His people, cleansing them from all sin, energizing them for all service, and guiding them through all circumstances as they make their way toward their heavenly inheritance, of which the Holy Spirit is the pledge and guarantee.

Truth at Work:

1. What is the Holy Spirit's connection with the world of *nature?*

2. What is the Holy Spirit's connection with the world of *persons?*

3. What is the Holy Spirit's role in *the mission of the church?*

4. Have *you* been filled with the Holy Spirit?

5

The Bible Speaks of Salvation

John wrote, "The Father has sent his Son as the Savior of the world" (1 John 4:14). On nearly every page, directly or indirectly, the New Testament identifies the work of Jesus Christ as salvation.

When Billy Graham's ministry first became a media event, and was being discussed in all circles of American society, someone wrote a petulant letter to *Time* magazine asking, "Just what is Billy Graham trying to save us from?"

The answer to that question was given long before any Baptist preacher existed or any news magazine was published. The answer was furnished by an angel from heaven, who said to Joseph, "[Mary] will bear a son, and you shall call his name Jesus, for he will save his people *from their sins*" (Matt. 1:21, italics added).

Ancient Israel rejected Jesus because they wanted to be saved from the Romans, not from their sins.

Modern people reject Him because they want to be saved from poverty, or illness, or loneliness, or political oppression, or social injustice, but not from their sins.

Jesus fed the hungry, freed the oppressed, healed the sick, and taught the ignorant—but He did not come primarily as a reformer, healer, or teacher. He identified the heart of His mission in a statement directed to a tax collector who had just found God: "The Son of man came to seek and to save the lost" (Luke 19:10).

Unless Jesus can be our Savior, He will not be our Teacher or Healer or Reformer or anything else—except our Judge. He refuses to be exploited by our perverse wills and selfish aims. We cannot prepare His agenda or dictate His mission. He has come to save us from sin, and it is that or nothing.

To Simon Peter, He said, "If I do not wash you, you have no part in me" (John 13:8). And to a group of would-be welfare-staters, Jesus said, "Truly, truly, I say to you, you seek me . . . because you ate your fill of the loaves. Do not labor for the food which perishes, but for the food which endures to eternal life" (6:26-27). He then went on to identify himself, in the light of His coming cross, as that eternal life. If He is shunned from our hearts, He will not fill our stomachs.

Jesus knows that our deepest need is not physical, emotional, political, or economic. As a famous American general once affirmed, at their bottom our problems are theological. We need to be right with God. Only then can we straighten out tangled relationships with other people and with things. Christ comes to us in the interest of our salvation from sin.

I. Salvation Is a Universal Provision

A. *God wills to save all.*

The Bible makes it clear that God's love embraces the whole world, not just a small elite group within the world. Through an Old Testament prophet God declared, "I have no pleasure in the death of the wicked" (Ezek. 33:11). And a New Testament apostle wrote, "God our Savior . . . desires all men to be saved" (1 Tim. 2:3-4).

If God wills to save all, why are not all saved? If God wills to save all, is not the death of any unsaved person a defeat for the will of God? No, because God does not will to save all—or any—unconditionally. He wills to save those who repent of their sins and trust in Jesus Christ. God does not shanghai anyone into His kingdom. He offers salvation to us in Jesus Christ, and those who accept are saved, but those who refuse are doomed.

Weeping over Jerusalem, Jesus said, "How often would I have gathered your children together as a hen gathers her brood under her wings, and you would not! Behold, your house is forsaken and desolate" (Matt. 23:37-38). Two phrases pierce to the heart of the tragedy: "I would have . . . you would not." God has conferred an awesome power of choice upon us, and He forever respects that freedom. He is not unwilling to save any, but some are unwilling to repent and believe.

On another occasion Jesus bluntly and sadly indicted His rejecters, saying, "You refuse to come to me that you may have life" (John 5:40). Their problem was not inability to come but unwillingness to come. He invited and they refused. They could have accepted.

God wills to save all who come to Jesus, and He wills to judge all who refuse to come. The will of God is never defeated by stubborn and defiant sinners.

B. *Christ died to save all.*

Describing the condition of the world, John wrote, *"The whole world* is in the power of the evil one" (1 John 5:19, italics added). Mankind's need for salvation is universal.

Describing the provision of the Cross, John wrote, "Jesus Christ the righteous . . . is the expiation for our sins, and not for ours only but also for the sins of *the whole world*" (1 John 2:1-2, italics added). The remedy He provided is just as extensive as the illness that threatens our destruction.

The Atonement is not limited. It is sufficient for the whole world. There is merit enough, and power enough, in the cross of Christ to save all mankind. "All have sinned" (Rom. 3:23), but "One has died for all" (2 Cor. 5:14). "Christ . . . died . . . for the unrighteous," and all were unrighteous (1 Pet. 3:18; Rom. 3:10). "Christ died for the ungodly," and all were ungodly (5:6; Eph. 2:12). "Christ died for our sins," and "all have sinned" (1 Cor. 15:3; Rom. 3:23). In the blood of Jesus Christ there is an ample and mighty provision to save all persons from all sin for all time.

Jesus Christ is "the Lamb of God, who takes away the sin of the world" (John 1:29). That is why the wrath of God upon the impenitent and unbelieving is called "the wrath of the Lamb" (Rev. 6:16). It is the wrath of rejected and outraged love. Men are condemned because provision was made to save them, but they refused the mercy God offered them in the death of Christ.

"He is able for all time to save those who draw near to God through him" (Heb. 7:25). There is no want of love, power, or merit in Christ! But those who refuse to draw near—who shun His love and cling to their sins—will not be saved. I have preached to all kinds of people in all kinds of places, but I have never preached to anyone anywhere that God did not love and Christ could not save. Sadly, however, I have preached to many who refused to open their hearts to Christ. He is never guilty of breaking and entering. He is a Savior, not a burglar. He comes only at our invitation.

II. What Is Universally Provided Must Be Personally Appropriated

How do we receive what Christ has provided? How do we experience personally what the cross-hung Savior had accomplished when He cried in triumph, "It is finished"? The answer of the Bible is "through faith."

"What must I do to be saved?" cried a stricken jailer (Acts 16:30). The reply of Paul and Silas was, "Believe in the Lord Jesus, and you will be saved" (v. 31). In his letter to the Romans, Paul declares, "If you confess with your lips that Jesus is Lord and believe in your heart that God raised him from the dead, you will be saved" (10:9).

Faith acts upon "the word of faith"—the gospel of the grace of God—which is addressed to us as promise. When we believe that promise we are saved.

A. By faith we are justified freely.

God "justifies him who has faith in Jesus" (Rom. 3:26). To be justified means to be forgiven and accepted by God, who thereafter treats us as if we had never sinned against Him. This blessed acquittal and adoption becomes ours, not by our works but by our faith.

We do not earn God's favor and fellowship. He bestows them as gifts. This heartening truth is set forth in a great passage from Paul's pen:

> Since all have sinned and fall short of the glory of God, they are justified by his grace as a gift, through the redemption which is in Christ Jesus, whom God put forward as an expiation by his blood, to be received by faith (Rom. 3:23-25).

God does not offer a cheap and easy forgiveness. He can be just and yet the justifier of those who trust in Christ only because Christ bore our sins in atoning death. The holiness of God and the majesty of law were honored in the very act by which salvation was made possible for undeserving sinners.

In another glorious passage we read, "The wages of sin is death, but the free gift of God is eternal life in Christ Jesus our Lord" (Rom. 6:23). Wages are earned, a gift is not. If we got what we deserved from God, we would be banished to hell forever. Instead, He gives what we could never deserve, a full pardon of all our sins and a place in His own redeemed family. The greatest "rags to riches" story ever told is nonfiction, the gospel of Jesus Christ!

Because justification is by faith, a sinner can be saved at the very time he hears the gospel. We do not have to wait until we "clean up our act." Just as we are when we learn of Christ, we can trust in Him and be immediately released from the penalty and power of sin.

Justification by faith does not mean that the justified can live rotten lives and remain in favor with God. Jesus came to save us from our sins, not in our sins. The fact that salvation is by grace does not give us license for disgrace. Scripture teaches that God justifies the ungodly, but it nowhere affirms that He justifies ungodliness.

At the very moment forgiveness occurs in the mind of God, a change also takes place in the heart of the believing sinner. He is born again. Birth is the beginning of life, and new birth is the beginning of new life. The pardoned sinner begins to live by new principles and walk in new directions. He now lives under the Lordship of Jesus Christ. The words of Christ to every forgiven sinner are, "Sin no more" (John 5:14; see 8:11; 1 John 3:4-10) and "Follow me" (Matt. 9:9; John 12:26).

B. *By faith we are sanctified wholly.*

Jesus prayed to the Father for the Church, "Sanctify them in the truth; thy word is truth" (John 17:17). Paul echoed that prayer, adding the significant adverb "wholly" (1 Thess. 5:23). We are to be made holy in body, soul, and spirit—made holy entirely. A good translation is "through and through." Paul coupled the petition with a promise: "He who calls you is faithful, and he will do it" (v. 24).

Across the centuries great numbers of Christians have run scared from that prayer and promise, managing to convince themselves that God cannot or will not do it. A woman in my home church used to come often to the altar of prayer, drawn there by a hunger for holiness. But she would not pray. She sat on the altar, folded her hands, looked defeated, and muttered, "It's too good to be true." No. It's too good not to be true! Those who believe enter into a glorious experience of being cleansed from sin and devoted to God.

The sin problem is twofold—the sins we have committed and the sin we have inherited. Committed sin must be forgiven, but inherited sin must be cleansed. This deep inward cleansing from all sin is provided in the blood of Jesus Christ. "Jesus also suffered outside the gate in order to sanctify the people through his own blood" (Heb. 13:12).

Christ is no partial Savior from sin. He offers an inward cleansing that enables us to love Him supremely and to love others unselfishly. "The blood of Jesus his Son cleanses us from *all* sin" (1 John 1:7, italics added). Sin is long-standing and deep-rooted, but the blood of Jesus Christ goes deeper than the stain of sin can reach.

The pure heart is a united heart. The Psalmist prayed, "Unite my heart to fear thy name" (Ps. 86:11). "Purity of heart," said a Christian philosopher, "is to will one thing." The cleansed heart no longer oscillates between Christ and the world. It is drawn to the will of God as a magnetic needle is drawn to the north pole.

David prayed, "Create in me a clean heart, O God, and put a new and steadfast spirit within me" (Ps. 51:10, margin). By the power with which He created the world, the Savior purifies the heart and anchors it to the will of God. The result is inward reinforcement against all the outward pressures that threaten to collapse the soul.

This purity and power are received by faith. The writer of Hebrews reminds us that the heart is "strengthened by grace, not by foods" (13:9). "Foods" is a reference to ritual meals, thought by some to produce inward holiness in an almost magical way. Christian rituals and Christian activities do not strengthen the heart. *The heart is strengthened by what God does for us, not by what we do for God, and the context identifies this strengthening grace as the sanctifying work of Jesus Christ* (vv. 10-12). What is offered as grace must be received by faith.

When the risen Christ summoned Paul to the task of preaching, He spoke of those who are "sanctified by faith" (Acts 26:18). The outpouring of the Holy Spirit upon the disciples at Pentecost "cleansed their hearts by faith," according to Simon Peter (15:9). Paul declared that God saves us "through sanctification by the Spirit and belief in the truth" (2 Thess. 2:13). We are not made holy by works, or by growth, or by death, but by faith.

There is a maturing process that produces an increasing likeness to Jesus Christ. This process is lifelong (2 Cor. 3:18; 2 Pet. 3:18). But the inward cleansing from sin, which is the negative side of sanctification, takes place in the moment one believes the promise of God to sanctify wholly. Growth is swifter and healthier after the cleansing has occurred and the heart is fixed upon the Lord.

John L. Brasher was the pastor of a large church in Birmingham, Ala. He attended a Salvation Army revival where Samuel Brengle was preaching. Later he confessed to being "charmed" by Brengle but aroused to "combativeness" by the messages on holiness. Nevertheless, Brasher hungered for a clean heart, and in an afternoon service he knelt at the penitent-form.

On one side of him knelt a bum, on the other side a streetwalker. Brasher confessed, "It was a bitter pill for the pastor of a large church, graduate of a celebrated school of theology, with some excellent prospects for the ministry, to be thus humiliated." As he prayed, God crucified his foolish pride and he entered into what he called "the Canaan of Perfect Love." Brasher's tremendous influence as a preacher and educator in the holiness movement dated from a moment of quiet faith at that disquieting altar.

Since faith is the condition for being sanctified wholly, the ball is in our court. God has made the provision and given the promise. The next move is ours. A leper came to Jesus, pleading, "Lord, if you will, you can make me clean." Jesus responded, "'I will; be clean.' And immediately his leprosy was cleansed" (Matt. 8:2, 3). The Lord wills cleansing from sin. His power is adequate to effect that cleansing. At the junction where our faith intersects His promise, the miracle of cleansing occurs.

The experience of being sanctified wholly is a gate and not a road. There is still the road to be traveled, and it is fraught with many dangers and difficulties. This fact leads us to another observation about the role of faith in salvation.

C. *By faith we are provisioned daily.*

"My God," said Paul, "will supply every need of yours according to his riches in glory in Christ Jesus" (Phil. 4:19). Those riches are measureless. The most sophisticated calculator known to man cannot total the resources of God. And those boundless supplies are pledged to the support and sustenance of His people!

This is not the promise of an easy way. Indeed, how could Paul, who endured great suffering for Christ, ever have written a guarantee of what is called today "the good life"? The gospel of comfort and affluence, so attractive to middle- and upper-class America, is not found in the New Testament. This very promise of the divine supply of every human need was penned from prison!

Sometimes we need *a rough stretch of road.* We need to be chastened and toughened. God isn't raising spoiled brats. "He disciplines us for our good, that we may share his holiness" (Heb. 12:10). The symbol of our Christian faith is a cross, not a cushion. God supplies courage, faith, and hope by which we endure hardships and scale mountains. These help us die to self-indulgence that we might live to His glory.

Sometimes we need *forgiveness,* and that is part of God's supply. John said of his first Epistle, "I am writing this to you so that you may not sin; but if any one does sin, we have an advocate with the Father, Jesus Christ the righteous; and he is the expiation for our sins" (1 John 2:1-2). To stumble and fall does not mean defeat unless we are willing to accept defeat. Instant forgiveness awaits instant repentance and faith, allowing us to continue the journey homeward without delay.

Sometimes our needs are *physical* or *financial.* Faith channels into our threatened lives the resources necessary to sustain us. But God sustains us for service, not in luxury. For the prophet Elijah, who lived by the word of God, there was bread and water during Israel's famine, but there was no medium-rare chateaubriand, no orange cake with coconut icing. Those who live selfishly and wastefully will find it hard, if not impossible, to exercise faith during times of adversity. The faithful will continue to have faith, and they will rejoice in the fulfillment of our Lord's promise, "I will never fail you nor forsake you" (Heb. 13:5).

Sometimes our need is *patience*—the courage to endure what God seems indisposed to change. The great faith chapter of the Bible, Hebrews 11, speaks of two kinds of faith.

One is *achieving* faith, which "conquered kingdoms, enforced justice, received promises, stopped the mouths of lions, quenched raging fire, escaped the edge of the sword, won strength out of weakness, became mighty in war, [and] put foreign armies to flight" (vv. 33-34). That is the kind of faith we like to shout about in camp meetings.

But the chapter speaks also of *enduring* faith. "Some were tortured, refusing to accept release, that they might rise again to a better life. Others suffered mocking and scourging, and even chains and imprisonment. They were stoned, they were sawn in two, they were killed with the sword; they went about in skins of sheep and goats, destitute, afflicted, ill-treated—of whom the world was not worthy—wandering over deserts and mountains, and in dens and caves of the earth" (vv. 35-38). How does that grab you? A cave-dweller for Jesus! Try to fit that into the gospel of comfort and pleasure being peddled on television!

Only the Lord knows what we need. Our wisdom is not that great, and if we call the shots we will forfeit the game sooner or later. Boiled down and skimmed off, faith is a trust in God that enables us to go right on serving Him no matter how unpleasant and puzzling our circumstances. Faith is all-weather and all-terrain equipment.

Continuing faith is necessary because salvation is a *process*. The meaning of salvation never lies wholly in past events. We "have been saved." We are "being saved." "We shall be saved." Paul used all three phrases, for salvation is both crisis and process—past, present, and future. The challenge of each new day, with its obstacles and opportunities, is "Have faith in God."

* * *

All have sinned and have incurred the righteous wrath of a holy God. From that predicament we are helpless to save ourselves. Jesus Christ has come to our rescue, reaching out to us a nail-scarred hand of mercy. When we place our hand of faith in His hand of grace, He lifts us into new life. The past is forgiven, the present is sustained, and the future is assured.

By simple trust in the sure mercies of Christ we can be freely justified, wholly sanctified, and daily kept. The process of being saved brings us over rough terrain at times, but our Savior never forsakes us. What He has commenced He continues and He will complete. He is the Savior of all who believe—who believe not as a mental exercise but as a volitional commitment.

Like Thomas of old, we may dissolve our doubts in His atoning death and confess, "My Lord and my God!" (John 20:28).

Truth at Work:

1. How does the death of Jesus Christ *differ* from that of *martyrs* such as the apostle Paul or Abraham Lincoln?

2. What are the implications for *changed behavior* in the biblical promises of salvation?

3. To what extent can we be saved from sin *this side of death?*

4. What is your personal experience of salvation *to this point* in your life?

6

The Bible Speaks of Christian Living

God has acted in Jesus Christ to save us from sin. The Holy Spirit is present in the Church and in the world to execute that provision of redeeming grace. At the time and place where we believe the promises of Scripture, salvation becomes ours in personal experience.

Our salvation is a lifelong process, and from the moment it begins we are involved in the serious, continuous responsibility of living for Christ in a non-Christian—and frequently anti-Christian—world. What God has wrought, we must express in daily lives of devotion to His will.

Paul charged the Philippians, "Work out your own salvation with fear and trembling; for God is at work in you, both to will and to work for his good pleasure" (2:12-13, italics added these verses). What God works in, we must work out. And how we do so is important too. God expects—and enables—joyful obedience, not merely mechanical compliance. Therefore, Paul's next words are, "Do all things without grumbling or questioning, that you may be blameless and innocent, children of God without blemish . . ." (vv. 14-15).

It is time now to look at this matter of Christian living. Once again, our subject is too vast for the few pages available

71

for it in this little book. But we will look at a few of the salient points taught in the Bible about the lives of Christ's people. They may be summed up in the three words *imitation, holiness,* and *love.*

I. IMITATION

To the church at Corinth Paul wrote, "Be imitators of me, as I am of Christ" (1 Cor. 11:1). A Christian should be like Christ. The attitudes and actions of Jesus should be reproduced in the lives of His followers. As Lord, He commands us to follow Him. As Teacher, He models for us the behavior patterns we are to establish in our lives.

When He had washed the disciples' feet, Jesus said, "I have given you an example, that you also should do as I have done to you" (John 13:15). The world will judge the Christian by the degree to which he is like or unlike Christ. Christian living is Christlike living.

This does not mean that we are saved by our efforts to follow His example. We are saved only by faith in the merit and power of His atoning death. But while we are being saved, we are instructed and obliged to live as He lived.

John wrote, "He who says he abides in him ought to walk in the same way in which he walked" (1 John 2:6). This is a very broad statement of responsibility that I once attempted to concentrate into three propositions, and I take the liberty of repeating them here.

A. *Jesus walked as a man contented with God's will.*

He could say, "I always do what is pleasing to [the Father]" (John 8:29). In the severest moral struggle of His entire life, Jesus prayed, "Nevertheless, not as I will, but as thou wilt"

(Matt. 26:39). He was unswervingly loyal to the will of His Father, even when He knew that the price of obedience would be death.

But Jesus was not only committed to God's will but also *contented* with it. He did it gladly, not grudgingly. "My food," He said, "is to do the will of him who sent me, and to accomplish his work" (John 4:34). As food satisfies the body, so the mind and spirit of Jesus was satisfied by doing the will of His Heavenly Father.

Paul came to that same position. He could write from prison, "I have learned, in whatever state I am, to be content. I know how to be abased, and I know how to abound" (Phil. 4:11-12). To walk as Jesus walked means "godliness with contentment," not whimpering or complaining in self-pity when our circumstances become difficult or dangerous.

B. *Jesus walked as a man devoted to others' needs.*

He summed up His earthly life in these words, "The Son of man . . . came not to be served but to serve, and to give his life as a ransom for many" (Mark 10:45). Peter supplied us with our briefest biography of Jesus: "God anointed Jesus of Nazareth with the Holy Spirit and with power; . . . he went about doing good and healing all that were oppressed by the devil, for God was with him" (Acts 10:38). Jesus spent His life, and finally sacrificed His life, in compassionate ministry to human needs.

We ought to walk in this same way. This is precisely how the apostles interpreted Christian duty. John writes, "If any one has the world's goods and sees his brother in need, yet closes his heart against him, how does God's love abide in him?" (1 John 3:17). And James wrote, "Religion that is pure and undefiled before God and the Father is this: to visit orphans and widows in their affliction, and to keep oneself unstained from the world" (1:27). To walk as Jesus walked means to serve the needs of the sick, the hungry, the unsheltered, the oppressed, the imprisoned, and the disenfranchised.

The Christ who would not work a miracle to feed himself did perform one to feed a hungry multitude. His life was not turned inward but outward. He did not demand service; He gave service because He cared deeply about people. His people should live unselfishly, too, as champions of the downtrodden and underprivileged.

C. *Jesus walked as a man burdened for earth's lost.*

The primary concern of His mission is focused in these words: "The Son of man came to seek and to save the lost" (Luke 19:10). Men were lost, away from God, in bitter slavery to sin, and in danger of perishing eternally. Jesus came to save them, like a shepherd questing through the night and storm to rescue lost sheep.

Moved by this same spirit, Paul declared, "I have become all things to all men, that I might by all means save some" (1 Cor. 9:22). Such intense concern for the lost should blaze at the center of every Christian life. To walk as Jesus walked will take us straight to lost sinners, to tell them of a Savior who can salvage them from sin and give them peace with God.

II. HOLINESS

To His Old Testament people, Israel, God said, "You shall be holy; for I the Lord your God am holy" (Lev. 19:2). To His New Testament people, the Church, He directs the same command: "As he who called you is holy, be holy yourselves in all your conduct" (1 Pet. 1:15). Holiness is, therefore, another way of describing the imitation of Christ.

The author of Hebrews tells us that "Jesus . . . suffered outside the gate in order to sanctify the people through his own blood" (13:12). We are familiar with that scripture, and most of us have heard many sermons preached from it. The verses that follow are not as well known, but they supply some helpful insights into the sort of living that flows from the sanctified heart. They speak of the holy life.

A. *The holy life is a **suffering** life.*

"Let us go forth to him outside the camp, and bear the abuse he endured" (v. 13). To follow Christ puts us on a collision course with the world. In this world we can expect abuse, reproach, and tribulation. "All who desire to live a godly life in Christ Jesus will be persecuted," affirmed Paul (2 Tim. 3:12). The extent to which believers suffer for Christ will vary from time to time and from place to place. Nevertheless, since the devil is "the ruler of this world" (John 12:31), some form and degree of suffering will be imposed upon all who have broken from his rule to live for Christ.

That "abuse" may come in the home or on the job. Sometimes it even occurs in churches. Whatever the source and whatever the force of reproach, the Christian is expected to endure mistreatment without retaliation. Peter and John, beaten by the Sanhedrin for preaching Christ, "Left the presence of the council, *rejoicing that they were counted worthy to suffer* dishonor for the name [of Jesus]" (Acts 5:41, italics added). They reflected the attitude of their Master, for "when he was reviled, he did not revile in return" (1 Pet. 2:23).

Holy life will be popular only with holy people, never with the ungodly and the worldly. If you think everyone will respect and appreciate you because you follow Jesus Christ, you will soon be disabused of that naive notion. "In the world," warned Jesus, "you have tribulation." Then He added, for our comfort, "Be of good cheer, I have overcome the world" (John 16:33). The world He overcame cannot overcome us as we trust in Him.

B. *The holy life is a* **seeking** *life.*

"For here we have no lasting city, but we seek the city which is to come" (Heb. 13:14). Christians are pilgrims. They are passing through alien and often hostile territory. But they are headed home, en route to "a better country . . . a heavenly one" (11:16). In that eternal city holiness will be commonplace. The ugly faces of sin, sorrow, and suffering never push in there. Nothing evil mars that society, but all is just and true and good. Crimes, riots, and wars will never devastate heaven. No illness, pain, death, or grief will sadden the hearts of its population.

With such a goal before them, drawing them on through thick and thin, Christians should never react to suffering with self-pity. Heaven will make all the trials we have endured just a drop in the bucket of human experience. God shall wipe away all tears from our eyes and all hurts from our memories, and we shall rejoice in His presence forever.

D. M. Coulson, one of our pioneer preachers, was witnessing to an unsaved cousin. Under conviction for sin, this cousin became angry, spit in his face, and snarled, "You holiness people are the scum of the earth." He smiled, wiped the spittle from his face, and replied, "Sister, have you ever noticed that scum always rises to the top?"

We who follow Christ are rising to the top. We are en route to "the city which has foundations, whose builder and maker is God" (Heb. 11:10). We are "seeking a homeland" (v. 14), and we shall not be disappointed.

C. *The holy life is a **sacrificing** life.*

Two kinds of sacrifices are mentioned in this passage from Hebrews. One is the sacrifice of *shared goods:* "Do not neglect to do good and to share what you have, for such sacrifices are pleasing to God" (13:16). Christians are to care for the hurting people all around them. Being Christian toward the needy involves more than gospel tracts and prayers. It includes mundane things like groceries and medicines and help with the chores.

When my mother died, I walked along the trails of memory recalling her life. From my earliest childhood I remember her busily helping desperate or lonely people. No hungry traveler was ever spurned from her door. No ill or injured neighbor was ever denied her tender nursing skills. No depressed or bereaved friend was ever compelled to weep alone. Day and night, often for weeks on end, she gave herself unsparingly to the needs of others. She made it impossible for me to believe in any profession of holiness that is not coupled with acts of charity and mercy.

The other sacrifice is that of *constant praise.* "Through him then let us continually offer up a sacrifice of praise to God, that is, the fruit of lips that acknowledge his name" (13:15). You cannot divorce holiness from happiness. Jesus said, *"Blessed are the pure in heart"* (Matt. 5:8). If and when and where our blessedness will inspire audible praise depends in part upon temperament and cultural conditioning. But this is sure—the Christian life is one of gratitude continually felt and expressed to God as the Author of all the benefits we daily receive.

According to the Psalmist, God is "enthroned on the

praises of Israel" (Ps. 22:3). That would be a tight squeeze in a lot of lives! Because goodness and mercy follow us all the days of our lives (23:6), praise should continually be in our mouths (34:1). No day should pass in which we do not offer unto God sacrifices of thanksgiving. The Psalmist also said, "I will give thanks to the Lord with my whole heart" (111:1). The unthankful heart is not whole. Spiritual health and peace inevitably inspire praise to God.

D. *The holy life is a* **submissive** *life.*

"Obey your leaders and submit to them; for they are keeping watch over your souls, as men who will have to give account" (Heb. 13:17). Obedience to God-constituted authorities is a mark of true Christian living. Disciples of Christ are not to be rebellious and anarchistic.

God has ordained structures of authority for the home, the church, and the state. Christians cannot reject these authorities, therefore, without incurring the displeasure of God (Rom. 13:1-2).

Does this mean that blind obedience is to be given to human authorities whatever the moral content of their commands? No, indeed! When the commands of men contradict the commands of God, we must obey Him and not them, accepting whatever consequences follow. To do evil at any person's bidding is to give that person the absolute obedience that only God should receive. When we absolutize any human authority we become guilty of idolatry.

A choice illustration of this principle is found in Acts 4:18-21. The apostles were commanded "not to speak or teach at all in the name of Jesus" (v. 18). They politely refused the order, saying, "Whether it is right in the sight of God to listen to you rather than to God, you must judge; for we cannot but speak of what we have seen and heard" (vv. 19-20). The Lord had sent them to preach and teach. His command to speak had precedence over the council's attempt to silence their witness. When human mandates clash with divine orders, "We must obey God rather than men" (5:29).

Unless and until human authorities contradict divine Lordship, we obey the Lord by obeying them. When such contradiction arises we obey the Lord by disobeying them.

John writes of a man named Diotrephes who "put himself first," refusing to acknowledge the authority of the apostle (3 John 9). Perhaps there is at least one such person in every local church! They must not be allowed to conquer and corrupt the family of God. "Jesus is Lord," and He chooses to exercise His Lordship through those who are called to teach and preach His Word. To reject their work is to oppose His will, and that is sin.

Between preachers and laypersons there should be a "partnership in the gospel" (Phil. 1:5). When we are all submissive to Christ we can then submit to one another without loss of dignity or worth. Indeed, in submission to those whom Christ sets over us, we find true liberation and fulfillment, not oppression.

In this matter Jesus Christ is our model, just as He is in other relationships. As a child, He was obedient to His parents (Luke 2:51). As a man, He was obedient to His Heavenly Father (John 15:10). "He learned obedience through what he suffered," and this obedience qualified Him to be "the source of eternal salvation to all who obey him" (Heb. 5:8-9).

True sonship is not essentially a legal or biological relationship. Sonship equals obedience to the will of God. Satan tempted Jesus, saying, "If you are the Son of God, command . . ." Jesus replied, "It is written . . ." (Matt. 4:3-4). The devil equated sonship with privilege, with the right to command. Jesus defined sonship as obedience, as freedom to submit to the Word of God. We will find nothing but defeat and misery if we operate from a demonic definition of sonship.

James exhorts, "Submit yourselves therefore to God. Resist the devil and he will flee from you" (4:7). Our resistance to evil depends upon obedience to God. We obey God when we submit to those authorities that He has placed over us in life.

Do you recall the words of Samuel to the arrogant and highhanded Saul? "To obey is better than sacrifice" (1 Sam. 15:22). No religious activity compensates for the stubborn rejection of God's clear Word. Rebellion, the prophet insisted, is as witchcraft—and practicing witchcraft was a capital crime in Israel. We keep the Word of God by our obedience to authority. The allowable exception occurs only when we must disobey authorities in order to keep the Word of God.

E. *The holy life is a **supplicating** life.*

"Pray for us . . ." (Heb. 13:18). Prayer is indispensable to Christian living. He who does not pray will not stand and will not grow. Prayer, as a poet put it, is the Christian's "native air." We can no more live for Christ without prayer than we can breathe mud.

Jesus was a man of prayer. He made times and places for communion with the Father. Whatever His company or activity, He gave priority to prayer (Mark 1:35; Luke 6:12). He prayed privately and publicly, and always sincerely. He prayed for himself and for others. According to Heb. 7:25, His ministry of intercession continues forever.

The servant is not above his Master. If prayer was vital to the life of Jesus, prayer is necessary for all His disciples. His first followers requested, "Teach us to pray"; Jesus responded, *"When* you pray, say . . ." (Luke 11:1-2). He did not say, *"If* you pray . . ." He assumed they would pray—a natural assumption, given the fact that holy living means likeness to Christ.

Everything crucial to our spiritual life, growth, and success is assured us when we pray in faith. "Whatever you ask in prayer, believe that you have received it, and it will be yours" (Mark 11:24). Whatever impedes or destroys faith will have the same effect upon prayer. Prayer is hindered by *sin* (Ps. 66:18); *pride* (Luke 18:10-14); *sloth* (James 4:2); *selfishness* (James 4:3); *rebelliousness* (1 Pet. 3:1-7); and an *unforgiving spirit* (Mark 11:25). Submission to God brings freedom in prayer, and prayer brings every needed blessing to our lives.

We are to pray at all times (Eph. 6:18), for all men (1 Tim. 2:1), and for all things (Mark 11:24). That sounds like prayer is indispensable to our lives!

A friend of mine was injured while plowing. Several ribs were broken. Taken to a busy hospital, he lay for hours on a gurney, unattended and unrelieved. His breathing was difficult and painful. Finally, in sheer desperation, he complained, "Lord, You ain't helping me!" The Lord answered, "You haven't asked me yet." "You're right, Lord," he admitted, "but I'm asking You now." Within minutes, he testified later, his pain abated and normal breathing was restored. "Ask, and it will be given you" (Matt. 7:7).

III. LOVE

"Love" is another way of saying "imitation of Christ" and "holiness." The essence of holiness is "pure love alone reigning in the heart." Christ walked in love and to emulate Him is to do all things from love.

81

A. *Love is likeness to Christ.*

There are no words more searching and challenging than these from the lips of Christ:

> *A new commandment I give to you, that you love one another; even as I have loved you, that you also love one another. By this all men will know that you are my disciples, if you have love for one another* (John 13:34-35).

In this same chapter of John's Gospel it is written of Jesus, "Having loved his own who were in the world, he loved them to the end" (v. 1). Not only were they in the world, but the world was in them as well. How unloving and unlovely they often were! One of them would soon betray Him, another would deny Him, and all would forsake Him when He most needed them. Nevertheless, He continued to love them. And His accepting, forgiving, and enduring love becomes the standard by which Christianity is judged. Such invincible love is the "badge of discipleship."

Jesus commands us to love the outsider as well as the insider.

> *I say to you, Love your enemies and pray for those who persecute you, so that you may be sons of your Father who is in heaven; for he makes his sun rise on the evil and on the good, and sends rain on the just and on the unjust. For if you love those who love you, what reward have you? Do not even the tax collectors do the same? And if you salute only your brethren, what more are you doing than others? Do not even the Gentiles do the same? You, therefore, must be perfect, as your heavenly Father is perfect* (Matt. 5:44-48).

This is how Jesus loved. From the Cross He gazed upon the heartless mob that mocked His anguish and prayed, "Father, forgive them; for they know not what they do" (Luke 23:34). His love was a flame that no flood of mistreatment and injustice could quench.

Loving as the Lord loves is what distinguishes between the real and the nominal Christian.

B. *Love is the fruit of the Spirit.*

Loving as Jesus loves is not "doing what comes naturally" but doing what comes supernaturally. It was natural for Him, for His very name and nature are love. But it is not natural for us whose hearts, apart from the surgery of divine grace, are selfish and stony. We can love friends and enemies alike only when "God's love has been poured into our hearts through the Holy Spirit which has been given to us" (Rom. 5:5).

Love is "the fruit of the Spirit," and is manifested in "joy, peace, patience, kindness, goodness, faithfulness, gentleness, [and] self-control" (Gal. 5:22). Only when self-will is crucified, and Jesus Christ reigns in our hearts unrivaled, are we able to bear the fruit of the Spirit in lavish and luscious measure. The fruit of the Spirit is a reproduction of the character traits of Christ. Only the power of the Holy Spirit is sufficient to prepare our hearts for the production of this fruit.

"The aim of our charge," said Paul, "is love that issues from a pure heart and a good conscience and sincere faith" (1 Tim. 1:5). No one can possess and express such love until the heart is pure, and only the Spirit of holiness can effect such inward cleansing. When He does, love becomes the master passion of one's life. Love determines attitudes, words, actions, and reactions.

C. *Love is active goodwill.*

Love is not sentiment, not emotion, but active goodwill. Jesus summarized the law in two commandments—Love God supremely and your neighbor unselfishly. Then He taught us how to define *neighbor*, and what it means to love our neighbors, by telling the story of the Good Samaritan (Luke 10:25-37). The neighbor is the person who needs our help, the hurting victim. Loving the neighbor means giving that help by sharing our resources. The story closes with the command, "Go and *do* likewise" (italics added these verses). Love is not content to feel for people; it *does* for them.

Love gives. "For God so loved the world that he *gave* his only Son" (John 3:16). "Christ loved the church and *gave* himself up for her" (Eph. 5:25). "Little children, let us not love in word or speech but *in deed* and in truth" (1 John 3:18). Love cannot be aloof or passive in the face of gaping wounds and glaring needs. Love must act, must give, must spend and be spent for others. And a love like Christ's will not allow artificial barriers of race, gender, culture, politics, or religion to set the boundaries of its doing and its giving.

Paul's charge to the Ephesians is God's word to us all: "Be imitators of God, as beloved children. And *walk in love,* as Christ loved us and gave himself up for us, a fragrant offering and sacrifice to God" (5:1-2). Make love your walk, not an occasional hop, skip, and jump between long stretches of selfishness.

*   *   *

The Christian life calls for some tough personal decisions. Ethical issues are not always clear-cut. Among Christ's people opinions differ and confusion arises. Precisely what it means to imitate Christ, to be holy, and to act in love in every specific situation may be the subject of hot debate and opposite conclusions. Who has the wisdom to prescribe for others in every case?

What we must do is maintain a stance of complete obedience to the Word of God as we understand it, seeking for light and making truth welcome. Convinced that a certain course of action is biblical, we must commit ourselves to it without condemning those who differ. Judgment should be left to Him whose right alone it is to judge.

Because we are never competent to judge even ourselves, we must cling to the gospel—the good news that we are forgiven, renewed, and cleansed by God's mercy and not by our merits. The sanctification of the justified never removes the need for the justification of the sanctified. Now and forever, we are saved by grace through faith in the atoning blood of Jesus Christ.

We must never forget, however, that the grace that reaches us to save also teaches us to serve.

> *The grace of God has appeared for the salvation of all men, training us to renounce irreligion and worldly passions, and to live sober, upright, and godly lives in this world, awaiting our blessed hope, the appearing of the glory of our great God and Savior Jesus Christ, who gave himself for us to redeem us from all iniquity and to purify for himself a people of his own who are zealous for good deeds* (Titus 2:11-14).

Truth at Work:

1. How can we know *what Jesus would do* in the various situations of our lives?

2. Why do equally earnest and devoted Christians sometimes arrive at *different conclusions* on moral issues?

3. How do we fix the *limits* of our obedience to *human authorities,* or should our obedience be unlimited?

4. What are *your* opportunities and responsibilities for Christian *social action?*